GOD IS IN
THE GLOVE COMPARTMENT

poetry and drawings by

Al Beck

minds nurtured by
curiosity: ultimate
aphrodisiac

discussion between two intimate pages of history

𝕷𝖔𝖗𝖎𝖊𝖓 𝕳𝖔𝖚𝖘𝖊

P. O. BOX 1112
BLACK MOUNTAIN, NC   28711

SOPRANO GROAN-A-PHONE

(makes a sound like one might emit
after Christmas celebrations are over
and one steps on the scale)

A passionate life
includes memorable,
arrogant glissando !

This book of poems and drawings
is dedicated to four special teacher/
friends in my life:
George Cohen
Bob Kinoy
George Kokis
Bill Stipe
who, each in their unique way,
shared this important thought:

the message is mightier
than the instrument
with which it is written.

autumn ends; gold leaves
tarnish. even birds of paradise
have off days.

GOD IS IN THE GLOVE COMPARTMENT

Perhaps somewhere else and at another
time I have told the story about our neighbor,
Mr. Wilson who took me to Sunday School
once when father was out of town. Mother
had not yet learned how to drive. We lived on
Asbury Terrace in Oak Lane, a suburb of
Philadelphia, PA. I was no more than a 4 year
old - or 5 at the most.
While he drove, we had this brief, important
discussion about God. What did HE look like?
Driving in his two-door Chevy coupe, he
seemed to come to the notion of a Supeme
Being from not so much a transcendent image
of God (up there . . . separate from us. . .
somewhere else) but from the immanent point
of view: "God is everywhere. God is in us and
in every part of the universe."
And I wondered as I heard him say this -
sitting in the front seat next to Mr. W, whether
God was also in the glove compartment of this
Chevy. And what was HE *doing* in THERE
for pity's sake? Without hesitation, I opened
up Mr. Wilson's Chevy glove compartment.

CONTENTS

book cover: floor motif from the Baptistery
in Florence, Italy -- scale: 1" to 2.625"

initiate our
imagination, we are
all snowflakes on fire

INTRODUCTION
AND ACKNOWLEDGEMENT

Three score and nearly nine years ago my mother brought
forth onto this continent a newborn urchin.

(spin around one more time, Abe)

I have been searchin' - rhyme notwithstanding -
for the ideal form of communication ever since:
First, it was with wet pants.
Then decorating childhood with spoken "shoulds
and shan'ts."
On to that pre-teen period of raves and rants.
Enter here the stage rejecting rhetoric for
unbridled gallivants.
A difficult age ensued of emotional gibberish
known as romance.
Afterward, discovered new languages in Korea
and then France.
Subsequently moved into the jargon of education
without a backward glance.
Then visual expression preceded serious linguistic
circumstance.

    Now, finally, culminating in these books of
    metric patter and verbal dance.
    And so in collaboration with my fingers'
    continuing conversations with clay, I have
    found some satisfaction on these levels of
    communication.

Haiku/Senryu is more than poetry with its very
strict limitations of form, rhythm and content.

It is also a state of mind in which the framework
is set for each reader to become a part of the
process.
Assisting the reader in this process are the
various sections within the book - playful,
curious, thoughtful, inscrutable, absurd, angry
and downright outright: Natural Force, Sylvan
Space, Human Discourse, Gravity's Grace,
Critical Resource, and Reflections Face. These
are insights of the author and may or may not
be taken literally, litterally or literarily.
Additionally, the drawings do attempt to be a
companion form with their own peculiar message
 - some with written description - some without.
Just as the potter enters into dialogue with the
vessel he or she is making, so too the poet becomes
the vessel from whence emerges the contents'
existence. The experiences are remarkably similar.

I owe a great deal of gratitude to six brave
Reaction Readers: Renee Gorrell, Dick Holmes,
Georgeann Perrotti, Ruth Ellen Porter, Ellie
Rauscher and Ralph Rogers.
Each provided me with fresh insights into
how the haiku/senryu held up under their
thoughtful consideration.
David Wilson comes in for a well-deserved bow
of appreciation. As the editor/publisher for
Lorien House, he devoted much time to the
design of this final product.

THOUGHTS ON FORM

The Haiku is a vest-pocket form of poetry.
Actually, not all are identified as Haiku.
Senryu* is a similar style which also appeared
in Beaucoup Haiku and now, again, in God Is
In The Glove Compartment.
Both use the 17 syllable - three line form. Both
are diminutive without losing their impact.
In fact, these poems give definition to elegant
and penetrating thoughts about nature, the
seasons, and the human condition (senryu).
Their origins in the Japanese 5/7/5 ideal form
now appear in a slightly more flexible internation-
ally-practiced structure. the distinction between
haiku and senryu lies in the former's focus on
"what-when-where" - whereas, senryu tends to
express human "who-what" ideas.

Terse Verse

Imagery in these miniature poems depends upon
contrasting and, simultaneously, complementary
expression. Irony, humor, satire, pathos. . . all
the range of observation is here. Beyond the
ubiguitous fortune cookie commentary, Haiku is
a complicated poetry form. As opposed to a
prolonged video production, it has single photo-
graphic image-impact.
In other words, these poems intimate or imply
rather than narrate or report. The reader is
charged with the task of connecting and entering
into the various layers of meaning. The impact may
or may not be subtle.

* * * * * * *

I believe I may be the first to use the word
"Flashpoint" as it refers to haiku/senryu poetry.
Flashpoint is a term identifying a series of haiku
or senryu where each poem has an attitude unleashed.
Select pieces would fall into this special category.

Definition:

FLASHPOINT is the recognition of ancient verbal
martial arts expressed through the haiku/senryu
poetry form. It is expression less like an explosion
than an incision. "Sound Bites" are contemporary
commercial corruptions of the Flashpoint concept.

* This form was originally introduced to me by David Priebe, Editor
of Haiku Headlines, a publication in which several of the poems in
this book have been previously published. A few others appeared in
my earlier books, Gnomes & Poems, Sight Lines, Songs From The
Rainbow Worm and Beaucoup Haiku.

HAIKU: mining for   acquired taste

Poetic Epiphany –

words, thoughts and phrases.

NATURAL FORCE

Nature's secret like
liquid laughter threads its way
just beyond our reach

bare feet in a moving stream.
Which is more affected --
feet or water?

rational fantasy --
leap from earth's ancient scars
to galaxies' stars

Fossils are footprints:
Time past trod. We curmudgeons?
-- current specimens

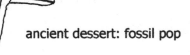

ancient dessert: fossil pop

we all experience
an Odyssey where search
becomes sacrifice

give thought to nature's
invective: poetic reflective
on thunder

lightning escorts
thunder to a dance -- with
predictable argument

raw wind's muscle
transforms rain shower into
angry, drenching body

storms where lascivious
leaves fly off the tree -- drown
in earth's dark power

STORM (couple)

vicious snarling storm beast
tears up sky's furniture --
thunder snaps and roars

* * * * * * * *

body-wrenched lightning bites.
drenched. no tender shower this !
God's sloppy kiss

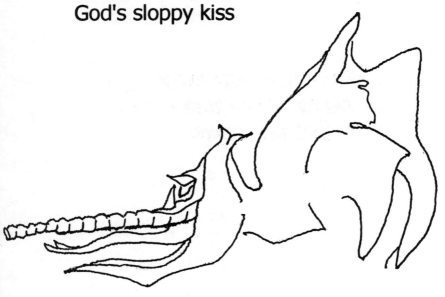

maintaining imperious distance

Flash claws skyline;
Thunder rip-cracks and roars;
Wet cat cowers in corner

white cat -- gray morning.
monochromatic look.
tail gingerly swishes

drizzle before daybreak --
sun rose without fanfare
-- God's feast or fiat?

naughty cat Dawn
slips daylight behind dark cloud;
purr-loined promise's shroud

cat's tongue -- a tiny
rake. bathes its fur coat better
than my dry cleaner

nest making, cat works
paws into my groin. what's worse
his claws or his drool?

sun slices youth's face
in warm shadow -- Spring arrives
with reckless bounce

heart's brisk beat: no soft
flutter from these April wings --
wild turkey sweeps low

I'm thinking about
the ax blade perfumed with
the wood it cuts into.

Spring has its own smell:
redolence of well-grounded
hope -- of raw spirits.

humans' twisted
history reveals Nature's
passion -- or maybe not

though Spring may switch on
our psyche, Time wires us to
asthenic circuits

pregnant mommy flower

to believe in
mystic force beyond our
peculiar nature, plant seeds

the soft spring rains
like wishes' wet velvet fingers
massage my shoulders

toast soundless
celebrations; silence is power
in ceremony

rain's rattle,
contrapuntal thunder --
nature-tympany crescendo

black wings surround the
wounded dinosaur -- dying
beast still arrogant

low line of thunderclouds
bulging dark bellies --
lightning-scarred sky beneath

touch night clatter's pulse:
rich, drenching rain-rattle
lightning's lick, crack and growl

rain and wind wrestle
accompanied by thunder's
bellow. vicious storm

rain's roof symphony
countless wet fingers practice
their percussion part

lightning bounces on
night sky's blanket -- cosmic
cavalier attitude

sky bares its teeth in
sudden torrent . . bites roof with
millions of raindrops

mired in silence,
fog bites the day -- arriving
unsteady on her feet

critters with wings which
flicker inevitably
shape shadows quicker

butterfly on dog's dish
ain't dialectics makin'
the puppy howl

butterfly pooping on flower it rejected

God showers us with
evidence of miracles --
watch bumblebees fly

butterfly lights on
fossil brought back from creek.
nature's ancient eye winks

Butterfly bomber - secret anthropomorphic weapon

July into August --
slathering sunlight. Summer
turns the corner

September sheds summer's
harvest angst. July's juice
is autumn's nectar

what happens to its leaves when a plant holds its breath

taste winter in
September's cool evening dance
God's gourmet thinking

Earth's sweet liquid spirit
settles back to its roots
when winter first bites

twilight -- the undetermined
distance distinguishing
dark from darker

Night: we fools stare at
stars before looking down at
what we're standing on

October shakes its
tambourine to glowing
crimson-umber voices

reforming. some shape
changes only occur when
the clay is ready

season's end -- milkweed
pods and me -- we wrinkled
old things still standing tall

lights dim -- devoured
by toxic gloom, winter
depression ossifies

winter's woven bare
branches -- warp into sky's
azure weft: accomplished

beyond human
uniqueness, snowflake designs
are nature's DNA

SYLVAN SPACE

I am astonished
at how snow's radiance
also dazzles the mind

high wind in November's
woods. dead oak down. leafless
trees: frantic dancers

wet winter woods --
umber/ochre leaf bed.
Rain for bloom. Rain for decay

My Old Playground

leaf tapestry gone.
November woods is now an
empty tangled warp

At four this morning
bony branches silhouette
the western gray sky

moonlight brushpaints the
footprints of woodland creatures --
shadow and silver

staring into shapeless
night past saplings' ghosts,
beyond stars or dark thoughts

sunrise. frost on the
roof. say goodbye to October's
color party

holiday bird with ornament

in morning darkness
owl wakes complaining. heard
me yell at barking dog

Squirrel up there somewhere
Hickory shells loudly spank
the deck. Cat's eyes stare

dressed for October's
party, sugar maples dance
to lively wind band

October's woodland
umber-leaf carpet; proud
of its natural pile

hairy dog plays in
autumn woods. comes home burr covered:
a walking bush

September signals:
exhausted summer green wears
orange on its edge

some weeds grow flashy
leaves with shallow roots;
others, deep roots one flower

walk on woods' well-worn
path. what prompts the spider
to hang its trapeze there?

the woodland wears a
shabby coat -- puddles and leaves:
September's children

Still morning air --
the lick of cool velvet.
Cow's moo wrinkles the silence

sunrise sparkles
dew-heavy spider's strand
perishable pearl necklace

cool August morning's
kiss? a mosquito tickles
my arm -- risks quick death

juicy jewels in the
underbrush -- arms scratched raw
picking blackberries

shishitou peppers
small pendulum fruit groom
in August green to red

blush too compelling
to resist. crabapples are
ready for harvest

winged insect's
soundless flight escapes new
sudden rain shower -- barely

Thumb-size crabapples
August polished, magenta
ripe -- young boys' weapons

Dare not clearcut these
precious commodities !
Trees are time's calendar

sweet rain in the woods:
soft sound, chaotic rhythm:
so mesmerizing

sky darkens. winds' wild
brush ripples pond a tight,
wrinkled design. Storm's blood

bird, frog, tree, wind
quartet -- backed up by thunder's
dark growl; nature's own jazz

storm lifts; light breeze bustles
woods left damp; mother fox
tussles with her cubs

wet leaf ground cover
reveals rejected nut
from squirrels' summer swarm

storm passes -- pond left
with shimmering fresh surface.
how it makes me smile !

sounds when rain stops:
last drops slip-tickle high leaves
to low; roof drip; pond plop

sounds of summer dawn --
frogs plop plop in the lake;
startled snake's hiss; my yawn

cows in meadow --
dawn sentinel silhouettes
against dull rose sunrise

rainclouds dark curtain
shuts out sunset's light;
sky meets land horizonless

in a moonless sky
so dark, we seine for stars;
wonder how they got there

sunset claws its way
through underbrush. less vindictive
breeze licks my face

Cottonwoods barely
shudder. Leaves' flattened petioles
spark their flutter

chestnut blossoms
in the hollow support
invisible hum; bee sharp !

how d'it get inside?
witness to bumblebee panic
door open. . .Shoo !

June frog in pond -- deep
throat croaking. Do I sound
like that in the shower?

cat's anguished wail
impolitely interrupts
warm night crickets' chorus

frog with brush

bullfrogs stir in
predawn's misty cloak; wish I
were conversant in croak

Daybreak. Night birds last
chatter. Frog talk. Distant dog.
Cat purrs in my lap

Full moon's faux sister
shamelessly reflects from pond.
Amused birds twitter

whizzing in the woods
by full moon; the stars don't
object so why should you?

Spring signals: among
dead leaves, green pregnant crocus;
snow's tattered patches

rain first detected
by rattle on leaves overhead;
then my wet skin

garden's first
asparagus sprouts are steamed
-- spring officially begins

red bud blooms blend with
white plum blossoms; early
spring's aristocracy

countless spring leaf-curtains
gently cover woodland's
clear winter window

end of March; crocus up,
daffodils budding --
grandstanding innocence

I watch the seasons
with affection as they
replace one another

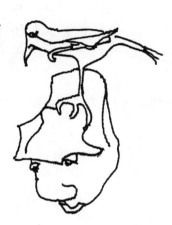

live in the woods --
overcome by Nature's gifts
and cruelty: yin. . . yang

outrageous lure

Tour jete by hybrid dancing worm

pixie admiring its elf-like
reflection in a shiny leaf

device to impale kvetchers

selective scrounger

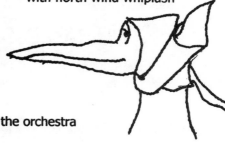

wounded goose
with north wind whiplash

conductor desperately signaling the orchestra
that he has to go potty

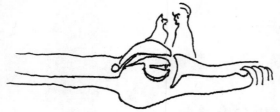

young boy discussing with his dog why
the alligator is wearing a stocking cap

shrike askew on a skate

Mr. Tealeaf reading himself

HUMAN DISCOURSE

Body, Mind, Spirit:
complex aspects; imponderable
chemistry

humans survive with
reason, humor and vivid
imagination

what chances for
bright mind, fair face and
body? Slim chance! Fat chance!

when dreams and memories
sometimes get confused . . well,
that's how it should be

fantasy transformation

muscles become
opaque when we wake but
sleep makes the mind translucent

peripatetic
iconoclast am I, who
sleeps with mental snakes

where did the night go?
I slept it through so undisturbed --
so unperturbed

Prince of Stagnation

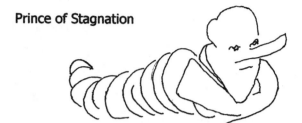

relationships
without empathy usually
breed apathy

love's early stage is
splayed confusion. age drains
the brains of what remains

love is that process
in which we search for soul
beneath the social skin

lovers sigh like a
furnace: romantic vertigo --
(more heat than height)

would ideal mate
anticipate partner's every need?
see dead frogs leap?

frog with walkman (aka: walkfrog)

until it grew some,
teenager mentality
was somewhat gruesome

Time is that lacy
web we first use as cradle,
then hammock, then shroud

Just when on this
fragile journey are we
answerable for our dreams?

jolted awake by
spider's unwelcome
delicate dance on my neck

feeling furry weight
in my lap. delay movement
for the cat's sake

mosquito lights on
my arm. swift death by hand/eye
coordination

wasp lands on my leg;
takes wing without sting.
one never shares too much luck

what moral voice urges
us treat both butterflies
and buzzards with care?

some people move through
our lives with a butterfly's
touch; others, a club

butterfly kiss

Our dog has human
lucidity moments -- or
are we projecting?

with ease cats contort
to clean splotches. we strain
wiping soap from our crotches

teenage moms
trade self-discovery to
perpetuate the species

she rose, -- shyly stepping
on the ashes which marked
paths of past regret

new age jewelry for the abidingly bashful

ours is a surface
connection. we are rooted
in separate soil

my child thinks we live
not in different worlds but
separate planets

people with fire
inside live by both its light
as well as its shadows

desensitized and disconnected

collecting adds weight
to life's adventure -- be it
myth or memory

talk to myself.
occasionally reasonable
conversations

mind chamber's wall draped
in memories' voice; floor --
layered with Life's meaning

cheers will shift into
lower gears as life inclines
to its later years

accepting age's
physical encumbrances
is deep-mind's burden

wounded by psychic shrapnel

Testing memory's
function with age is a swim
in mental pudding

When blinded to Art's
process, pull both feet and ego
from product's goo

potters rarely retire.
they eventually drop
with a glazed look

handbuilt now-broken
bowl repaired -- cracks invisible
-- almost. mine too

word-purgatory:
living on intellectual
faultline's edges

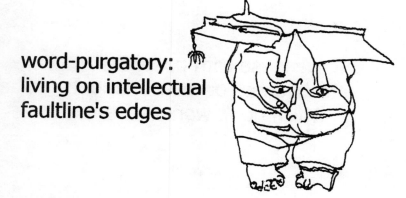

intellect with questionable body of knowledge

lost but lying
to yourself, convinced any
direction is Truth? Dance!

live loose with possible
effectiveness or measurements
which don't work

Idiosyncratic
teachers, hear this! -- Invention
involves doing !!

gone; the groves of our
early kin's time -- replaced by
huge human forests

early pre-bow hunting
power: extraordinary
atlatl

essential exercises --
stretching is second only
to laughing

devote years to pain
for brief Olympic moment?
human enigma

morning exercises

appetite and
energy dance apart --
too old to swing like Tarzan

he sported his
character like a glittery
Halloween costume

to remove sweater
quickly and not pull one sleeve
inside out. dream on

bureaucracy:
lizard, its tail cut off;
unworried, grows another

lizard handstand

mind unmoored,
imagination floats into
flowered estuaries

unlike Youth's acrobatics,
Age swims in a sacred
memory pool

Fire from Prometheus:
hear Future's music in your head.
Burnt shadows

painful memories
repressed meant sacrifice for
future investment

Life: maintaining balance
between adulation
and aggravation

please commemorate
my life as neither paradigm
nor parody

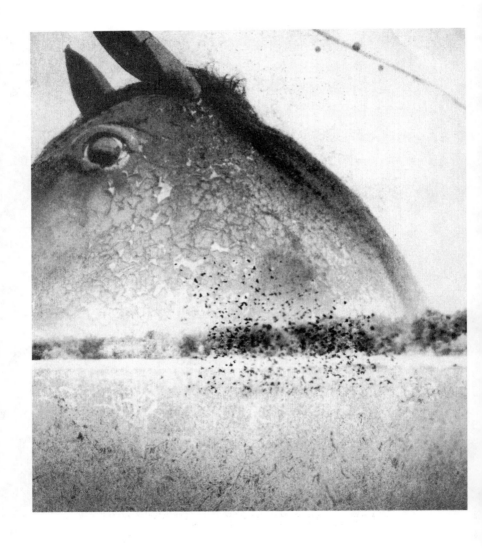

horse known as Apocalypse

madness begins within the fingers

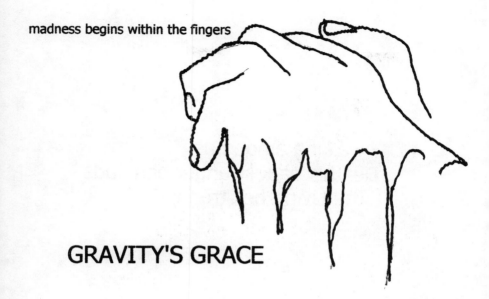

GRAVITY'S GRACE

to deny Death's deep
touch is silent protection
from ultimate grief

Life, like sucking an
ice cube, diminishes on
Time's wet tongue. (Don't bite!)

walking among us
Death's dark stranger demands
the Living be stronger

in the space/time
continuum either die or
outrun the demons

devil duck dancing

Survive parents' flaws;
search deep inside to discover
Destiny's claws

thinking about my
grandmother who would have
loved me had she known me

Death gathers the
living together. Disoriented,
we ask "Why?"

passing through,
directionless, rarely do I see
my mortal compass

at least we're headed in the same direction

passions for functional
formula produce
predictable products

kids conform -- psyches
    sucking video-combat;
right brain erosion

In life at some point
we turn useless -- confusing
elder with teen years

initial stages of confusion

with wounds from all
seasons, age carries its scars
of youth's exuberance

Meanspirited wear
shredded self-righteousness
under contentious clothes

savage temper:
anger so hot it blisters lips;
hate breeds violence

petulance

holy cloak drycleaned;
politician quickly sheds
his velcro values

flying petulance

beyond survival --
gaudy superficial vision
haughty humans !!

incompetence is
the arrogant mind suffering
from hubris

unfit leadership
gives Incompetence license
to birth Arrogance

some educators
fight change -- protected by
academic armor

learned Luddites be
aware: nineteenth century
reason is over

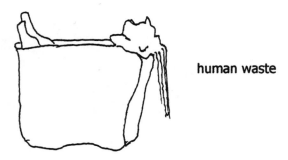

human waste

bureaucracy's
infectious kinship -- drawn to
submission by babel

education
continues stereotype-trapped --
disingenuous

politicians
massage language shaped into
mental silly putty

byzantine politics
of academia --
it isn't pretty

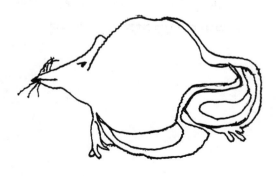

curlicued shrew

sensible lives, too,
marinate hate. social
vultures clean up the mess

middle management
like bottom feeder lobsters
eats whatever dies

suspicious at how delicious

Lost Perspective --
orphan of Antagonism
and False Assumptions

equivocation?
bad taste in my mental mouth.
wounded perspective

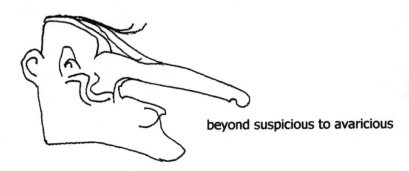

beyond suspicious to avaricious

passionless reason?
evidence of divine spark
better left buried

absence of proofs
empirical nurtures
excessive blind ritual

life, bearing savage
hole, shapes one's morality:
passion without soul

Will I endure such
brazen pain, yet not emerge
this dark maze insane?

greasy levels of dissatisfaction personified

curse broad strokes of
a sword which impales innocent
and guilty alike

lacking apology's
part, lessons in humility
turn lethal

Guilt: torment vehicle
chasing wounded ghosts.
Regret: -- the scar tissue

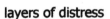

layers of distress

true pain may linger
in mind; but reflected in
eyes, lives long in heart

traditionally,
yesterday's tears are delicious
anguish. not mine

time in the mind --
descend into Black Rhapsody's
pool -- cruel ecstasy

mourn History's regrets;
revile thought which generates
their repetition

angry animal assuming
his vasectomy had been successful

clearcutting - industry's
pollution; Nature doomed
by human ambush

Art, not science, is
a bridge for our human
connection to Divine

vision frozen in
time and space: more suited
to discomfort than pain

human curse --
    color blind gardener can't tell
    when tomatoes are ripe

reflection defines
either Truth's illusion or
thoughtful confusion

garden marker for depressed plants

schemes nestled in brown
cedar needles: life needs more
  light to sustain it

Imagination's
voice: its ungoverned resonance
Power's Truth tool

Projection is Life's
trip we lunatics take to
distort Delphic Truth

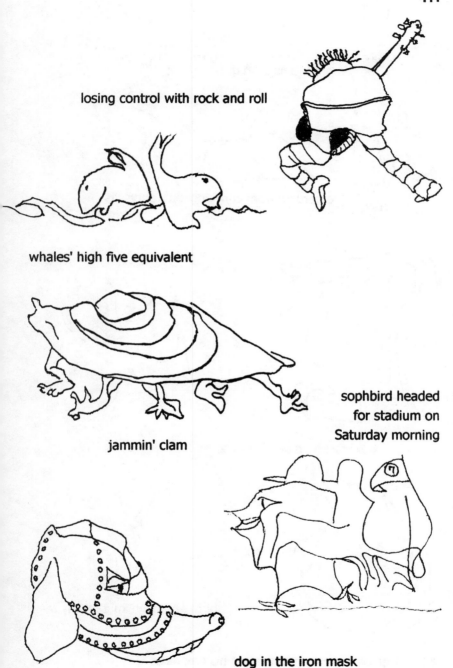

losing control with rock and roll

whales' high five equivalent

jammin' clam

sophbird headed
for stadium on
Saturday morning

dog in the iron mask

more brains than drawn

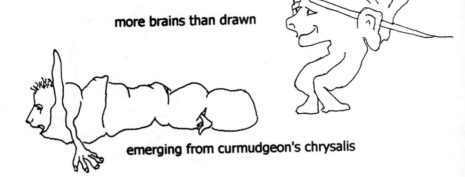

emerging from curmudgeon's chrysalis

boxer with upsweep hairdo

birth anomaly? mutant my tail !!

ancient greek jester contemplating his omphalos

CRITICAL RESOURCE

Opportunity --
the beast with only one tether:
an embarking

Balance: Nature's struggle
to maintain diversity
without falling

I may not always
know where I'm headed; -- still
stride there with confidence

Perseverance and
Change are two unaccountable
phenomena

Life choice:
ritualistic addiction or
living open minded

with a choice between
cynicism or wonder-and-awe:
no problem

floating has its yin
and yang; depending whether
face up or face down

parents' life-gifts all
bubble up to the surface
in their appointed time

there is no tomorrow,
no yesterday. we live
one smile at a time

Passion's playful fire
will surely singe the fringe of
Time's tattered carpet

History's not worn out
space but lavishly appointed
padded rooms

Shroud-wrapped silence
since my childhood enchantments
when movies were a dime

wise minds avoid
uniform solutions to
complex human problems

alternative
attitudes attract attention
to new solutions

all decisions are
circumscribed by a person's
limited vision

visually impoverished?
pack your palette with
complex color

new ideas, like
some seeds, germinate best
in History's compost

the first person to
observe rain probably
didn't know what it was

most victims of impatience
choose between comfort
and desperation

question: when running
in the rain do more drops hit
us than while walking?

Driving home. Vengeful
dark clouds slither by. God's in
the glove compartment

more than hear rain's
intensity; feel its downpour
in deeper places

resolve Life's doubts:
use the alchemy how we
feel about what we know

didactics:
artificial standards' refuge
or wrestling paradox

intellect without
creativity and
compassion: dangerous

creative thought states:
"there are no right answers
but plenty of wrong ones."

creativity
an elastic, fantastic
weapon sans equal

mind music and
mind Muse-ic both connect
horizon to fingertips

tooting one's own horn has its drawbacks

imagination
provides passion to remain
in the universe

build passion to
electric energy levels:
cosmic equipoise

when art's not
introspective, it remains
a superficial skin game

nothing is darker
and deeper in the soul than
imagination

when you're lost in thought
any mental passage ought
to be a way out

reluctantly, blind
momentum carries me from
one day to the next

positive thinking
keeps whatever's boiling in
the pot from stinking

vision's Truth is
generally a crutch. distance
is more smell than touch

Time is a rubber band
with arbitrary stretching
capacity

reach beyond our
limited space. search for larger
connecting touch

Time locks Passion
in Resignation's chamber --
released by Fantasy

bottle up excess
energy. pour yourself
into passionate tasks

Curiosity's
discomfort foreshadows
intrigue's pain. Be boring

couch critter

urgent
indispensability begets
pretentious inertia

Progress is measured
by personal best -- not against
others' failures

Who can relieve
another's itch? No one knows
how long or hard to scratch

Despite things
reasonably spiritual,
no one is beyond need

I'm often moved by
unexpected, generous
presence of kindness

minds nurtured by
curiosity: ultimate
aphrodisiac

word play: understanding
the difference between
obscure and obtuse

diversity -- a
critical factor in
compatibility

friendship -- unlike
pharmaceutical prescriptions --
spiritual touch

REFLECTIONS FACE

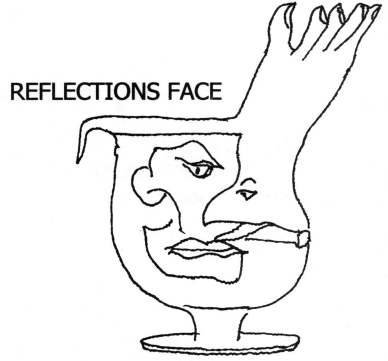

With change we fight it,
embrace it, or float with it --
face up or face down

Past: a dark, dangerous
diarrhetic in Present's
power for change

dragons joyfully
fly just beyond the edge of
earth - disconnected

Fate or Muse - Change's
message inevitably
out-reaches one's grasp

oddly enough,
a fish being a fish cannot
understand the sea

some mysteries,
unlike Gordian Knots, are
better left unraveled

cut into skin, deep
past the bone to where pain hides.
now I understand

recuperate
surgery -- leave flowers on
my chest, not a raven

mortar board bird with graduate tassle

honor our system
with ceremony at
Power's secular shrine

travel to Destiny;
rationalized facade;
surrounded by cats

Time is teacher at the
chalkboard. with ageless touch
she writes assignments

bitten by a wild
idea: teach us how to see
not what to see

which is more important:
the question we ask or
the answer we get?

Einstein's space and
Van Gogh's sky -- old truths and
novel possibilities

Time's merciless Truth
indispensable to our
human condition

Phoenix factor: place
where fruits of fantasy just
out of reason's reach

Life's best moments move
from senses to inner essence
. . . soul is nourished

lured by Immortality;
Fate victimized;
transubstantiate Truth

seek nexus with
incomplete ideas and
undiscovered passions

fresh phoenix from
yesterday's ashes -- healing
accommodates slowly

self control: bridging
the gap between featherbrained
and simpleminded

Fool . . .
irresponsibly obsessed with
Pythagorean perception

hand jester

child, five, racing down
hill of head-high corn.
indelibly nature-linked

Upon reflection,
at what point should I have cried
"Farewell Innocence!"?

examine Ritual's
corpse. note Curiosity's
dormant tissue

Curiosity's
thunder; passion in the air;
It's raining magic

wisdom is discovering
what synthesizes
passion with reason

idea's birth,
a paper-winged option, dies
during analysis

fraternal disorder

History
complicates newborn life as
each culture's knot unravels

it's insects not humans
choose smelly dung in which to
raise their young. Oooh?

whether Time's mattress
be firm, soft, thick or thin
depends on the ticking

ooze from the wound -- what
distinguishes History's
important moments

live briefly within
your borrowed body;
history honors the mind

Future's merged with Now;
many mental miles ahead
of reality

seek solution for
our labyrinth passage plight.
ask doppelganger

Question: is living
an interesting life a
blessing or a curse?

fish penetrates piscine fantasy figure

Creatures we in dreams'
deep sea -- Truth our bubbled wish;
green striped golden fish

be fantasies' flood
or mental trollop-dollop,
mind mud packs wallop

Don't photograph fleas
in moonlight without high speed
film unless they're dead

do the job well;
perfect revenge against
incompetent management

reflection is
Fortune's yearning for
overindulgence: Icarus

that far country where
we once met remains in my
mind a silhouette

at age six each week
is one year long; at sixty,
a year's one short week

space -- deep space:
Time's abyss of indifference
to who we really are

stubborn indifference

memories are less
intellectual snacks than
Time's strains or constraints

who are we but an
indecipherable parade
of past events?

what we use for our
protection often locks us
in masked whys. God sighs

keeping affection
at arm's length plays it safe;
but quarantines the heart

Are competition
and cooperation
culture's contradictions?

jungian janus creature

Passion to compete;
need to cooperate --
immersed in paradox

True Voice is found in
those random moments when
mind and feelings connect

harsh reality
is torn free from fringes of
woven fantasy

a leaf in dark shadow
may look like a rock --
life's little illusions

prayers' awesome silent
spaces are candles' bright bliss
in life's dark corners

curiosity,
like an incomplete sentence,
searches tasty thought

we know less about
human brains than what's put
into Chinese eggrolls

at some point with
activity, process takes on
a life of its own

not cliché but
sterility will kill culture's
design direction

companionship's
two gold coins: affection and
compatibility

God once told me
"Blind intuition is
 passion's greatest enemy."

morning stretch for the varsity kvetch

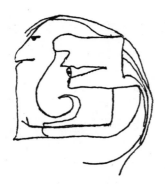

Shadow of the Cryptic Muse

dancing dodo

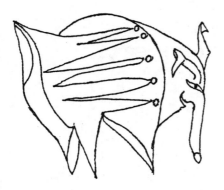

Flagtailed Feekus
(three legged, long nosed psyche sniffer)

man with an ill-fitting super ego

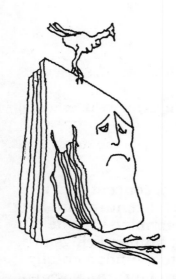

Dreaded feathered cynic shredder
tears holes in History

snail dude

moon rising above an upset stomach

NEGLECTED ESSENCE OF RESOURCEFUL SCHOOLS

(The Milking Stool Metaphor vs the stool we're milking)

It's time to infuse the milking stool concept into the
institutional learning process. 21st century thinking
about education will certainly determine the fate of
Humanity's direction. Presently, human beings are
connected to an educational system fundamentally
promulgated primarily by Western culture's social
phenomenon known as competition.
Grading procedures, honor roles based exclusively
upon GPAs, introduction to athletics (sports emphasis,
as opposed to physical education), best dressed, most
likely to succeed, best looking, smartest, fastest,
something-est; long before the 19th century mono-
exploitation strategy relying on the philosophy of
Sports Pharisees, "Winning isn't everything, it's the
only thing!" is proving to be a disaster in the learning
environment. Results? Intellectual incontinence.
The milking stool concept clearly connects three strong
legs to the seat of social influence. Competition is only
one of these. The other two are Cooperation and
Creativity. At this time, in Education, Competition runs
the ship. Cooperation is given a second class berth and
Creativity is rarely mentioned as a passenger in edu-
cational steerage. We must remember the anatomy of
Imagination is a foundation for human growth and
social harmony.

In her remarkable book, The Three Faces of Mind, Elaine de Beauport writes: "For me, the most urgent priority is to begin courses in multiple intelligences. At present most educational systems hope that the student will learn to think by following and memorizing the content of different subjects over a period from twelve to sixteen years. We do indeed learn a wide variety of content in many subjects but we never become conscious of the learning process involved. . . necessary change in education is to add the intelligences of the right hemisphere to the already existing rational intelligence of the left hemisphere."

The American Dream is clearly based upon the Free Enterprise notion which does not rely solely upon the competitive practice presently acknowledged to be the primary focus of our formal learning patterns.

If John Dewey were alive today you would have heard him remark that Education has become an irresistibly blunt force meeting an improvable, unmovable object. Build any functional structure without at least three "legs" it will remain upright temporarily until it eventually loses its balance. It's why pogo sticks are an uncommon form of transportation.

Even some primitive pre-human had to invent a "grub stick" to reach into the hole and bring out those delectable critters.

Despite the ubiquitous ancestral growls from education, new discoveries in human expression continue to flourish. Some will rationalize that without the rigid program from which to rebel, the creative soul would not emerge [nonsense from the established Gestalt camp]. The flaw in our thinking process lies not in the current effort to improve physical skills and intellectual substance but to ignore the equally inherent need to recognize, then develop, curiosity and imagination as essential life

forces. The shortcoming in education's traditional
philosophy is the premise that in order to become
creative one must "break the rules".

In a microchip society, we have placed such an
emphasis on production and technical prowess, that
the groundwork has been laid for the demise of the
human condition as we think we know it. There is no
other concept more prepared to deal with this critical
condition and perhaps even reverse the trend than the
milking stool metaphor.

If we don't watch out, we humans may become
tomorrow's casualty on the last babble-ground:
the Super Information Highway; ie: reactionary roadkill.
Traditional teachers often remain the natural predator of
the creative mind and cooperative concept.

Let's not even speak about the few who rely on formula
thinking to satisfy the needs of myopic principles
(aka: principals). Sooo, how many teachers have I
alienated at this point? And why in Heaven's name
would I involve this article in such pejorative accus-
ations?

In Robert Wright's book The Moral Animal (Why we are
the way we are: the New Science of Evolutionary
Psychology) he commented that what pressure usually
generates growth and change is a hostile environment.
And that is the condition which exists in our educa-
tional system today (with or without firearms).

We are ready for some serious growth and change.
We must build a new world in learning constructed
with three critical tools: independent Creative Thinking,
a carefully constructed Competitive Attitude and an
essential Cooperative Spirit. Cooperation is defined
here as an activity umbrella for such positive social skills
as empathy and kindness. One must assume the devel-
opment of behavior beyond the basic issue of conflict
resolution.

It is critical we establish a <u>National Institute for Educational Innovation,</u> and structure three initial phases in developing systemic change:

Phase one: Experimental Learning Teams (ELTs) on all levels of formal education. There would be four team members: two interdisciplinary educators, an activity coordinator and a facilitator-counselor-coach.

Phase two: Student teams on all levels would be selected for creative/cooperative learning experiences.

Phase three: <u>ALL</u> teachers would be retrained for continued certification with Left Brain/Right Brain activities for students on every learning level in all disciplines.

It is time to ask some critical questions to those who will deliver the social/educational/economic/cultural leadership to their appointed places in the year 2025 and beyond:

Shouldn't every problem presented to a student have as its fundamental raison-d'etre the revelation and development of that person's Soul ?

Is Soul the most neglected aspect of young people today as we seem to exclusively zero in on each student's intellect?

In a society where violence, greed, power and their offspring – envy, jealousy and hatred – obliterate cooperation, and a fanatically negative-news media complicate human survival, does it make sense to raise up parsing sentences, memorizing dates and drawing two-point perspectives as the building blocks for developing a new, sensitive generation?

Will information gathering and analytical thinking continue to be the primary focus in the soul of the learning process?

Time's peculiar structure
wraps our wounded framework
with precious wisdom.

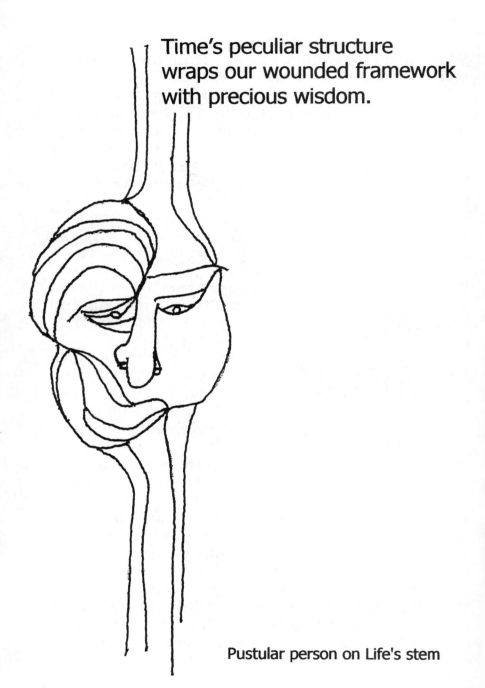

Pustular person on Life's stem

ABOUT THE AUTHOR

AL
BECK

Artists who work in a medium where the product
may or may not be either pretty or provocative are
part of a group of image makers who go beyond

superficial decoration as the function of their work.
Whatever medium Al Beck uses, poetry, clay, fabric
design, photography, pencil, folksong, papercasting
or compost, the art forms confront the viewer by
sending up personal flags, opening up taboo boxes
and sometimes even piercing minds with a visual
or verbal knife.
There is a playful vulgarity and irreverence for
conventional expectations.
His focus is to wed the personal expression to the
universal cry for a connection of our human spirit
to our intellect. Al believes that if we forget the
best part of ourselves expressed in visual arts, music,
poetry, dance and drama, then truly we will become
a cultureless society, and a nation of unfeeling
savages.

I've not yet come to terms

with age -- to detach -- be

released from its grip

BOOKLIST

"Al Beck is witty, playful, and having fun with words. If comparisons are fruitful, some of these poems reminded me of a giddy Ogden Nash."
- Dr. Sam Grabarski

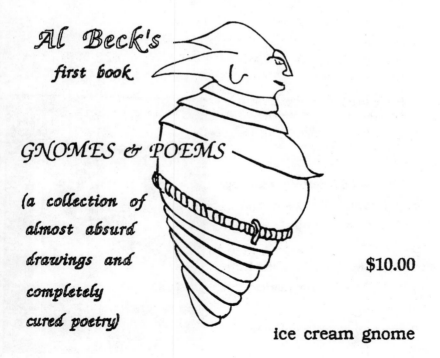

Al Beck's
first book

GNOMES & POEMS

(a collection of
almost absurd
drawings and
completely
cured poetry)

$10.00

ice cream gnome

SIGHT LINES

poems and drawings

by

AL BECK

$6.00

"Beck poems are delightful - full of life with no strained metaphors ! My husband enjoyed them, too. We found ourselves laughing aloud and reading poems to each other - not a frequent occurrence !"

Nola Ruth, Executive Director of Missouri Association of Community Arts Agencies.

SONGS from the RAINBOW WORM
Poems, Drawings, Photographs and Ceremonial Masks
by Al Beck

$9.50

"Al Beck's book features a number of poems and illustrations that truly reflect the author's wisdom and awareness."

Leo Shunji Nishida, Publisher /Editor, The Plaza, a quarterly dedicated to "space for global human relations." Published in Tokyo, Japan.

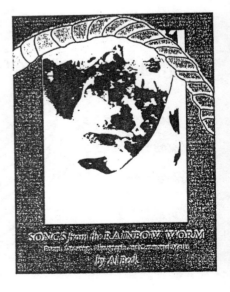

BEAUCOUP HAIKU
by Al Beck

BEAUCOUP
HAIKU

by AL BECK

$ 10.00

"Al Beck captures life from the side-door that most have thought was closed for good during the latest renovation. Part Woodstock, part Pete Seeger and part Gary Larson, he weaves his pen at a level that is just a bubble or two from plumb, but challenging, interesting and usually quite hilarious"...

John Tripp, Vice President
Denman Corporation

"Something here for everyone. Beck writes with an eye toward spiritual resonance, a blending of heart and spirit expressed in poetry. A veritable symphony of lyrical images and feelings !"

Dr. Dan Campagna   Playright/Professor

postpaid from: **Al Beck**
5987 County Road 231
Monroe City MO 63456

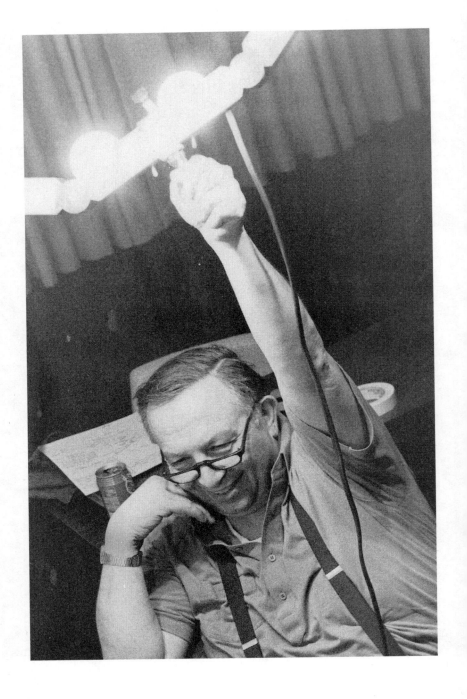